I0408310

Exhibit 1. Firearms Manufactured (1986-2014)

Calendar Year	Pistols	Revolvers	Rifles	Shotguns	Misc. Firearms[1]	Total Firearms
1986	662,973	761,414	970,507	641,482	4,558	3,040,934
1987	964,561	722,512	1,007,661	857,949	6,980	3,559,663
1988	1,101,011	754,744	1,144,707	928,070	35,345	3,963,877
1989	1,404,753	628,573	1,407,400	935,541	42,126	4,418,393
1990	1,371,427	470,495	1,211,664	848,948	57,434	3,959,968
1991	1,378,252	456,966	883,482	828,426	15,980	3,563,106
1992	1,669,537	469,413	1,001,833	1,018,204	16,849	4,175,836
1993	2,093,362	562,292	1,173,694	1,144,940	81,349	5,055,637
1994	2,004,298	586,450	1,316,607	1,254,926	10,936	5,173,217
1995	1,195,284	527,664	1,411,120	1,173,645	8,629	4,316,342
1996	987,528	498,944	1,424,315	925,732	17,920	3,854,439
1997	1,036,077	370,428	1,251,341	915,978	19,680	3,593,504
1998	960,365	324,390	1,535,690	868,639	24,506	3,713,590
1999	995,446	335,784	1,569,685	1,106,995	39,837	4,047,747
2000	962,901	318,960	1,583,042	898,442	30,196	3,793,541
2001	626,836	320,143	1,284,554	679,813	21,309	2,932,655
2002	741,514	347,070	1,515,286	741,325	21,700	3,366,895
2003	811,660	309,364	1,430,324	726,078	30,978	3,308,404
2004	728,511	294,099	1,325,138	731,769	19,508	3,099,025
2005	803,425	274,205	1,431,372	709,313	23,179	3,241,494
2006	1,021,260	385,069	1,496,505	714,618	35,872	3,653,324
2007	1,219,664	391,334	1,610,923	645,231	55,461	3,922,613
2008	1,609,381	431,753	1,734,536	630,710	92,564	4,498,944
2009	1,868,258	547,195	2,248,851	752,699	138,815	5,555,818
2010	2,258,450	558,927	1,830,556	743,378	67,929	5,459,240
2011	2,598,133	572,857	2,318,088	862,401	190,407	6,541,886
2012	3,487,883	667,357	3,168,206	949,010	306,154	8,578,610
2013	4,441,726	725,282	3,979,570	1,203,072	495,142	10,844,792
2014	3,633,454	744,047	3,379,549	935,411	358,165	9,050,626

Source: ATF's Annual Firearms Manufacturing and Exportation Report (AFMER).

[1]Miscellaneous firearms are any firearms not specifically categorized in any of the firearms categories defined on the ATF Form 5300.11 Annual Firearms Manufacturing and Exportation Report. (Examples of miscellaneous firearms would include pistol grip firearms, starter guns, and firearm frames and receivers.)

The AFMER report excludes production for the U.S. military but includes firearms purchased by domestic law enforcement agencies. The report also includes firearms manufactured for export.

AFMER data is not published until one year after the close of the calendar year reporting period because the proprietary data furnished by filers is protected from immediate disclosure by the Trade Secrets Act. For example, calendar year 2012 data was due to ATF by April 1, 2013, but not published until January 2014.

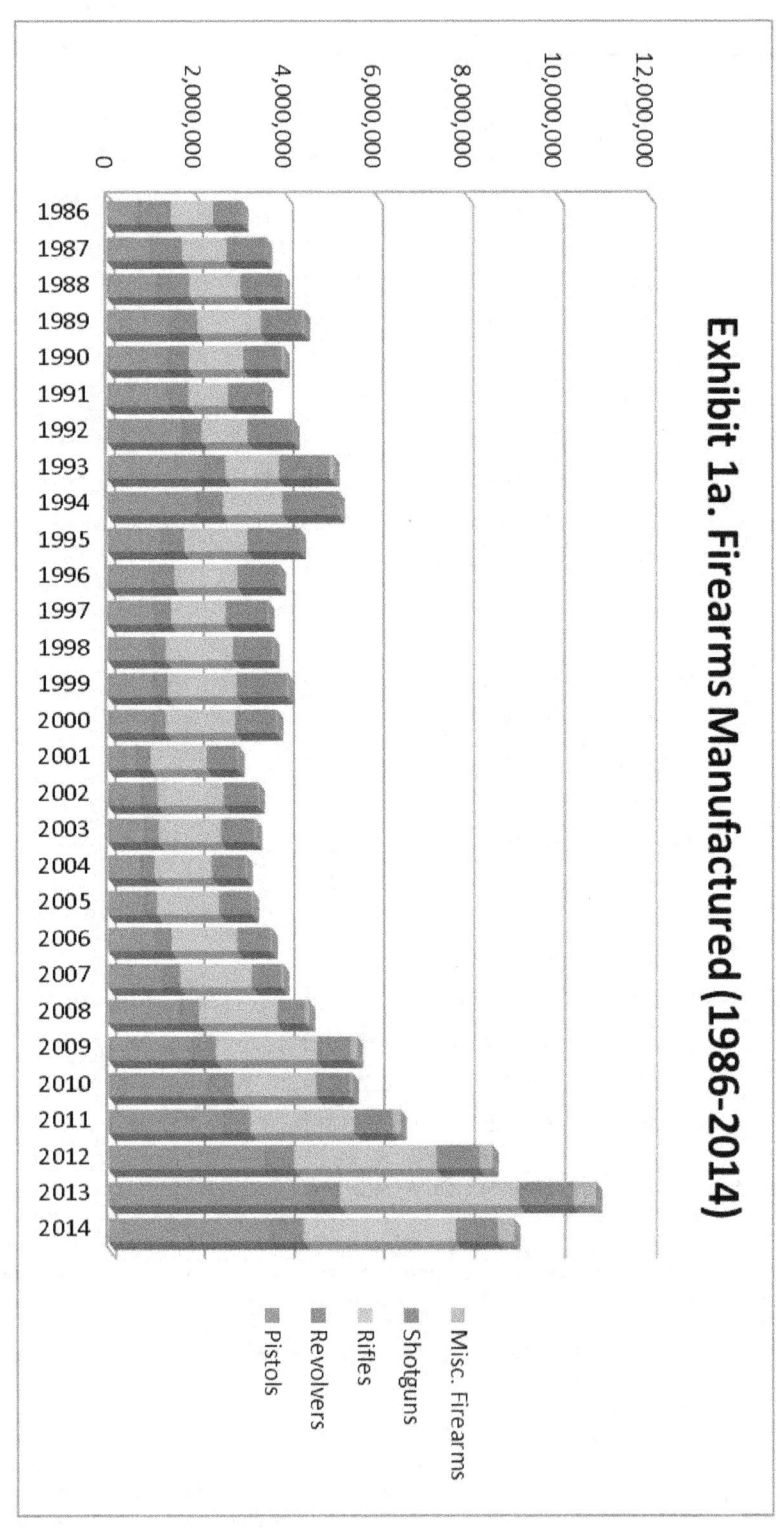

Exhibit 1a. Firearms Manufactured (1986-2014)

Exhibit 2. Firearms Manufacturers' Exports (1986 - 2014)

Calendar Year	Pistols	Revolvers	Rifles	Shotguns	Misc. Firearms[1]	Total Firearms
1986	16,511	104,571	37,224	58,943	199	217,448
1987	24,941	134,611	42,161	76,337	9,995	288,045
1988	32,570	99,289	53,896	68,699	2,728	257,182
1989	41,970	76,494	73,247	67,559	2,012	261,282
1990	73,398	106,820	71,834	104,250	5,323	361,625
1991	79,275	110,058	91,067	117,801	2,964	401,165
1992	76,824	113,178	90,015	119,127	4,647	403,791
1993	59,234	91,460	94,272	171,475	14,763	431,204
1994	93,959	78,935	81,835	146,524	3,220	404,473
1995	97,969	131,634	90,834	101,301	2,483	424,221
1996	64,126	90,068	74,557	97,191	6,055	331,997
1997	44,182	63,656	76,626	86,263	4,354	275,081
1998	29,537	15,788	65,807	89,699	2,513	203,344
1999	34,663	48,616	65,669	67,342	4,028	220,318
2000	28,636	48,130	49,642	35,087	11,132	172,627
2001	32,151	32,662	50,685	46,174	10,939	172,611
2002	22,555	34,187	60,644	31,897	1,473	150,756
2003	16,340	26,524	62,522	29,537	6,989	141,912
2004	14,959	24,122	62,403	31,025	7,411	139,920
2005	19,196	29,271	92,098	46,129	7,988	194,682
2006	144,779	28,120	102,829	57,771	34,022	367,521
2007	45,053	34,662	80,594	26,949	17,524	204,782
2008	54,030	28,205	104,544	41,186	523	228,488
2009	56,402	32,377	61,072	36,455	8,438	194,744
2010	80,041	25,286	76,518	43,361	16,771	241,977
2011	121,035	23,221	79,256	54,878	18,498	296,888
2012	128,313	19,643	81,355	42,858	15,385	287,554
2013	167,653	21,236	131,718	49,766	22,748	393,121
2014	126,316	25,521	207,934	60,377	784	420,932

Source: ATF Annual Firearms Manufacturing and Exportation Report (AFMER).

[1]Miscellaneous firearms are any firearms not specifically categorized in any of the firearms categories defined on the ATF Form 5300.11 Annual Firearms Manufacturing and Exportation Report. (Examples of miscellaneous firearms would include pistol grip firearms, starter guns, and firearm frames and receivers.)

The AFMER report excludes production for the U.S. military but includes firearms purchased by domestic law enforcement agencies.

This exh bit does not include statistics related to the National Firearms Act (NFA).

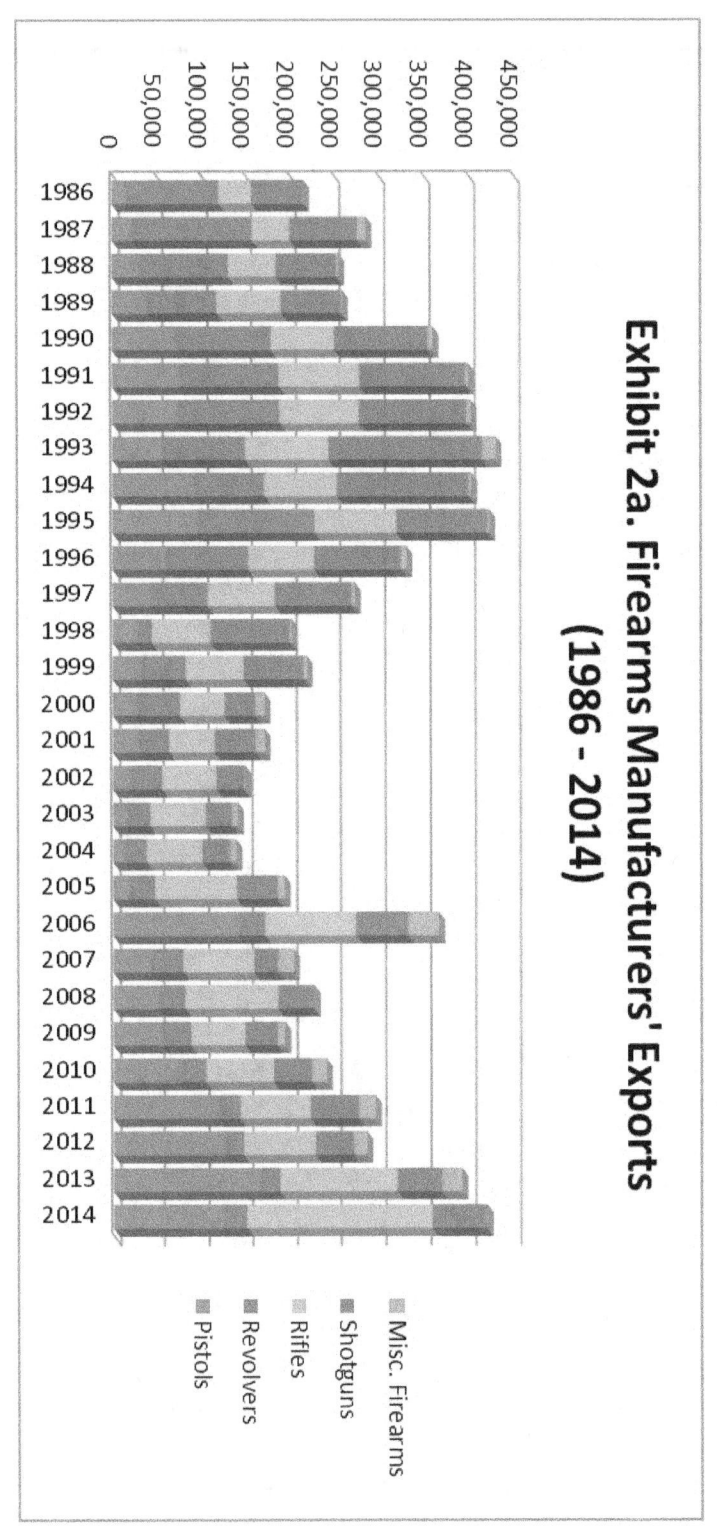

Exhibit 2a. Firearms Manufacturers' Exports (1986 - 2014)

Exhibit 3. Firearms Imports (1986 - 2015)

Calendar Year	Shotguns	Rifles	Handguns	Total
1986	201,000	269,000	231,000	701,000
1987	307,620	413,780	342,113	1,063,513
1988	372,008	282,640	621,620	1,276,268
1989	274,497	293,152	440,132	1,007,781
1990	191,787	203,505	448,517	843,809
1991	116,141	311,285	293,231	720,657
1992	441,933	1,423,189	981,588	2,846,710
1993	246,114	1,592,522	1,204,685	3,043,321
1994	117,866	847,868	915,168	1,880,902
1995	136,126	261,185	706,093	1,103,404
1996	128,456	262,568	490,554	881,578
1997	106,296	358,937	474,182	939,415
1998	219,387	248,742	531,681	999,810
1999	385,556	198,191	308,052	891,799
2000	331,985	298,894	465,903	1,096,782
2001	428,330	227,608	710,958	1,366,896
2002	379,755	507,637	741,845	1,629,237
2003	407,402	428,837	630,263	1,466,502
2004	507,050	564,953	838,856	1,910,859
2005	546,403	682,100	878,172	2,106,675
2006	606,820	659,393	1,166,309	2,432,522
2007	725,752	631,781	1,386,460	2,743,993
2008	535,960	602,364	1,468,062	2,606,386
2009	558,679	864,010	2,184,417	3,607,106
2010	509,913	547,449	1,782,585	2,839,947
2011	529,056	998,072	1,725,276	3,252,404
2012	973,465	1,243,924	2,627,201	4,844,590
2013	936,235	1,507,776	3,095,528	5,539,539
2014	648,339	791,892	2,185,037	3,625,268
2015	644,293	815,817	2,470,101	3,930,211

Source: ATF and United States International Trade Commission.

Statistics prior to 1992 are for fiscal years; 1992 is a transition year with five quarters.

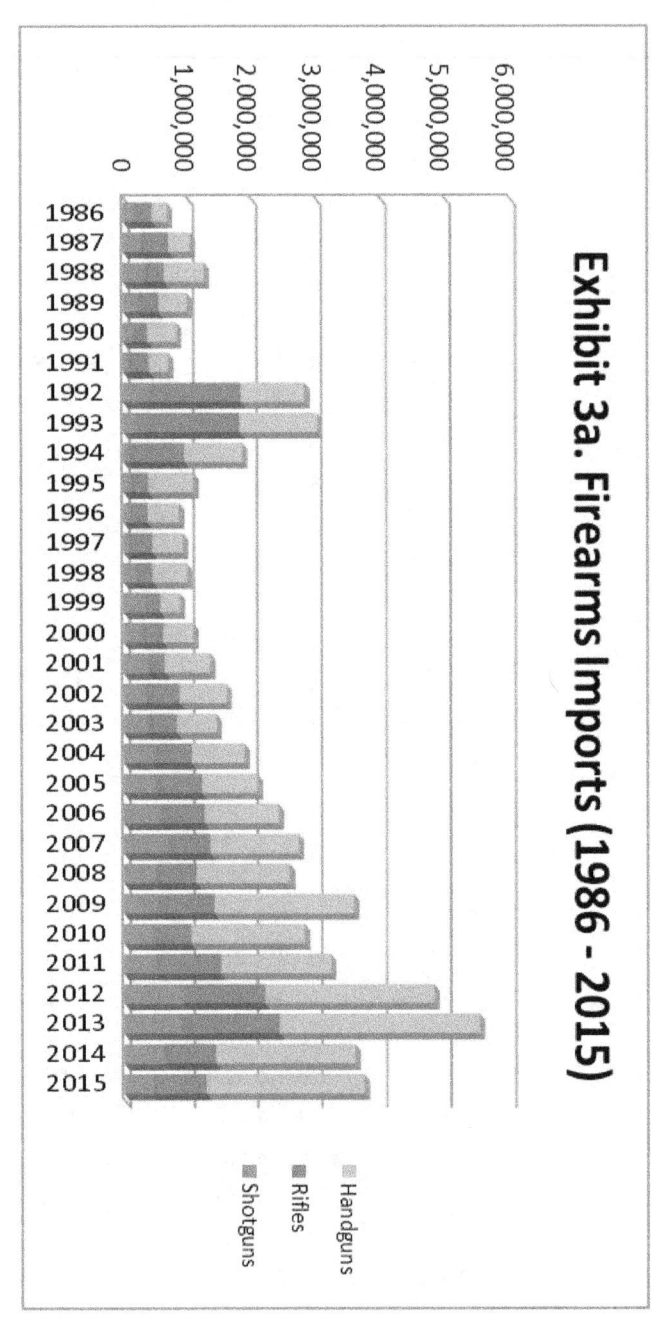

Exhibit 3a. Firearms Imports (1986 - 2015)

Exhibit 4. Importation Applications
(1986 - 2015)

Fiscal Year	Licensed Importer	Military*	Other	Total
1986	7,728	9,434	2,631	19,793
1987	7,833	8,059	2,130	18,022
1988	7,711	7,680	2,122	17,513
1989	7,950	8,293	2,194	18,437
1990	8,292	8,696	2,260	19,248
1991	8,098	10,973	2,412	21,483
1992	7,960	9,222	2,623	19,805
1993	7,591	6,282	2,585	16,458
1994	6,704	4,570	3,024	14,298
1995	5,267	2,834	2,548	10,649
1996	6,340	2,792	2,395	11,527
1997	8,288	2,069	1,395	11,752
1998	8,767	2,715	1,536	13,019
1999	9,505	2,235	1,036	12,776
2000	7,834	2,885	1,416	12,135
2001	9,639	3,984	1,569	15,192
2002	9,646	6,321	3,199	19,166
2003	8,160	2,264	2,081	12,505
2004	7,539	1,392	1,819	10,750
2005	7,539	1,320	1,746	10,605
2006	8,537	1,180	1,505	11,222
2007	8,004	1,081	1,236	10,321
2008	7,610	718	980	9,308
2009	7,967	504	970	9,441
2010	7,367	823	1,088	9,278
2011	7,647	641	959	9,247
2012	8,408	420	895	9,723
2013	9,964	319	597	10,880
2014	8,529	255	429	9,213
2015	6,078	318	897	7,293

Source: ATF Firearms and Explosives Import System (FEIS)

Import data excludes temporary permits issued to nonimmigrant aliens.

*Depicts ATF Form 6A Part 2 (5330.3C)

Effective April 8, 2014 Import permits are valid for two years.

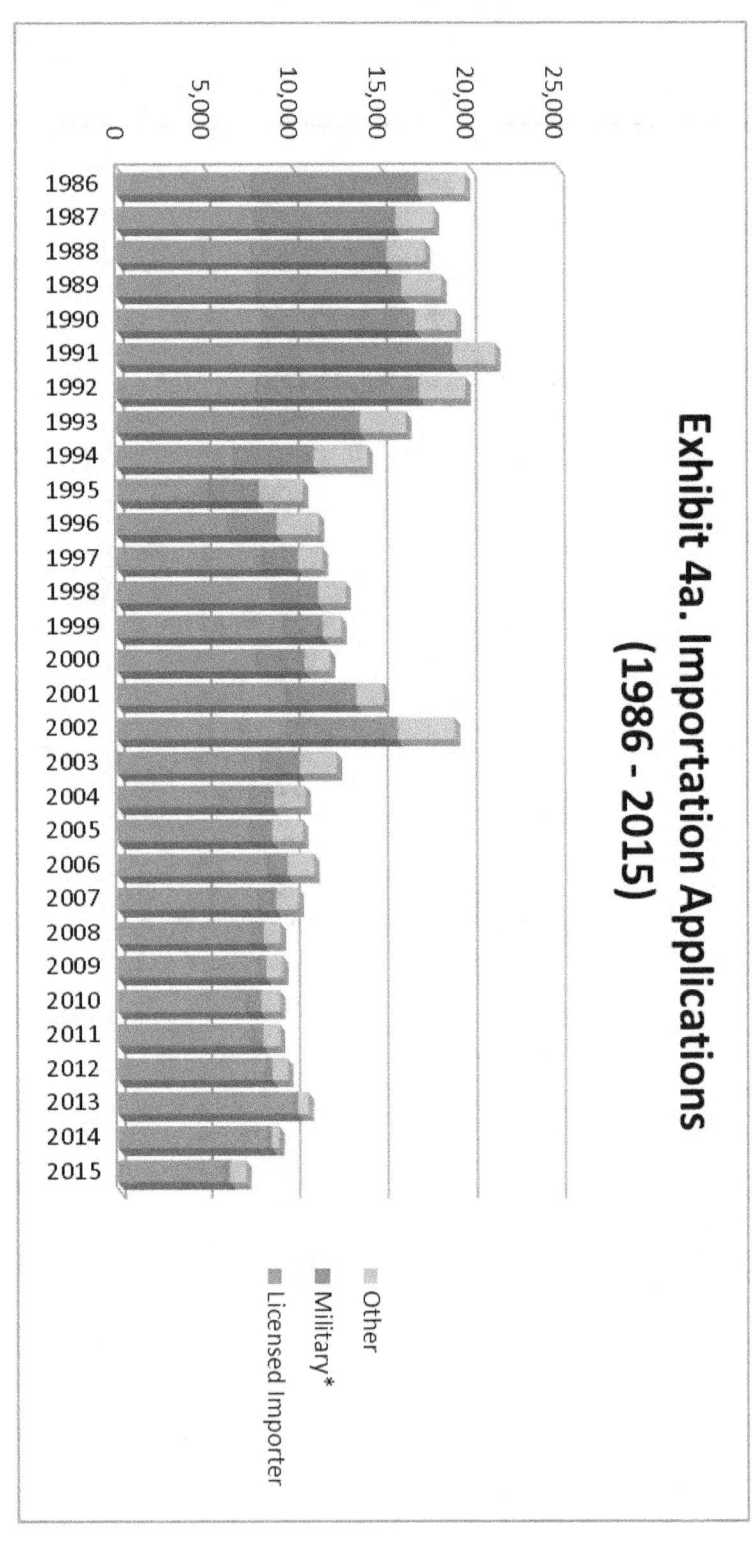

Exhibit 4a. Importation Applications (1986 - 2015)

Legend: Other, Military*, Licensed Importer

Exhibit 5. Firearms Imported into the United States by Country of Manufacture 2015

	Handguns	Rifles	Shotguns	Total Firearms
Austria	923,951	1,867	716	926,534
Brazil	485,639	78,585	38,225	602,449
Croatia	338,535	0	0	338,535
Canada	3,417	334,268	192	337,877
Italy	107,940	27,222	199,266	334,428
Turkey	80,939	339	220,310	301,588
Germany	236,935	17,651	1,536	256,122
China[1]	0	0	164,818	164,818
Czech Republic	76,029	28,181	109	104,319
Philippines	79,457	5,603	6,400	91,460
Japan	0	87,012	904	87,916
Serbia	18,066	62,308	0	80,374
Belgium	18,679	54,497	713	73,889
Finland	0	50,481	0	50,481
Argentina	42,304	0	0	42,304
Romania	9,460	17,982	0	27,442
Spain	239	25,371	839	26,449
Israel	15,618	4,302	0	19,920
United Kingdom	7,419	4,687	578	12,684
Bulgaria	6,267	5,100	0	11,367
Poland	10,783	527	0	11,310
Russia	0	4,406	5,150	9,556
Switzerland	3,971	2,463	0	6,434
Portugal	0	2,117	4,175	6,292
Hungary	1521	27	0	1,548
Slovak Republic	1,075	0	0	1,075
Slovenia	1,058	0	0	1,058
Other[2]	799	821	362	1,982
Total	2,470,101	815,817	644,293	3,930,211

Source: ATF and United States International Trade Commission.

[1]On May 26, 1994, the United States instituted a firearms imports embargo against China. Sporting shotguns, however, are exempt from the embargo.

[2]Imports of fewer than 1,000 per country.

Imports from Afghanistan, Belarus, Burma, China, Cuba, Democratic Republic of Congo, Haiti, Iran, Iraq, Libya, Mongolia, North Korea, Rwanda, Somalia Sudan, Syria, Unita (Angola), Vietnam, may include surplus military curio and relic firearms that were manufactured in these countries prior to becoming proscribed or embargoed and had been outside those proscribed countries for the preceding five years prior to import. Imports may also include those that obtained a waiver from the U.S. State Department.

Imports from Georgia, Kazakstan, Kyrgyzstan, Moldova, Russian Federation, Turkmenistan, Ukraine, Uzbekistan are limited to firearms enumerated on the Voluntary Restraint Agreement (VRA).

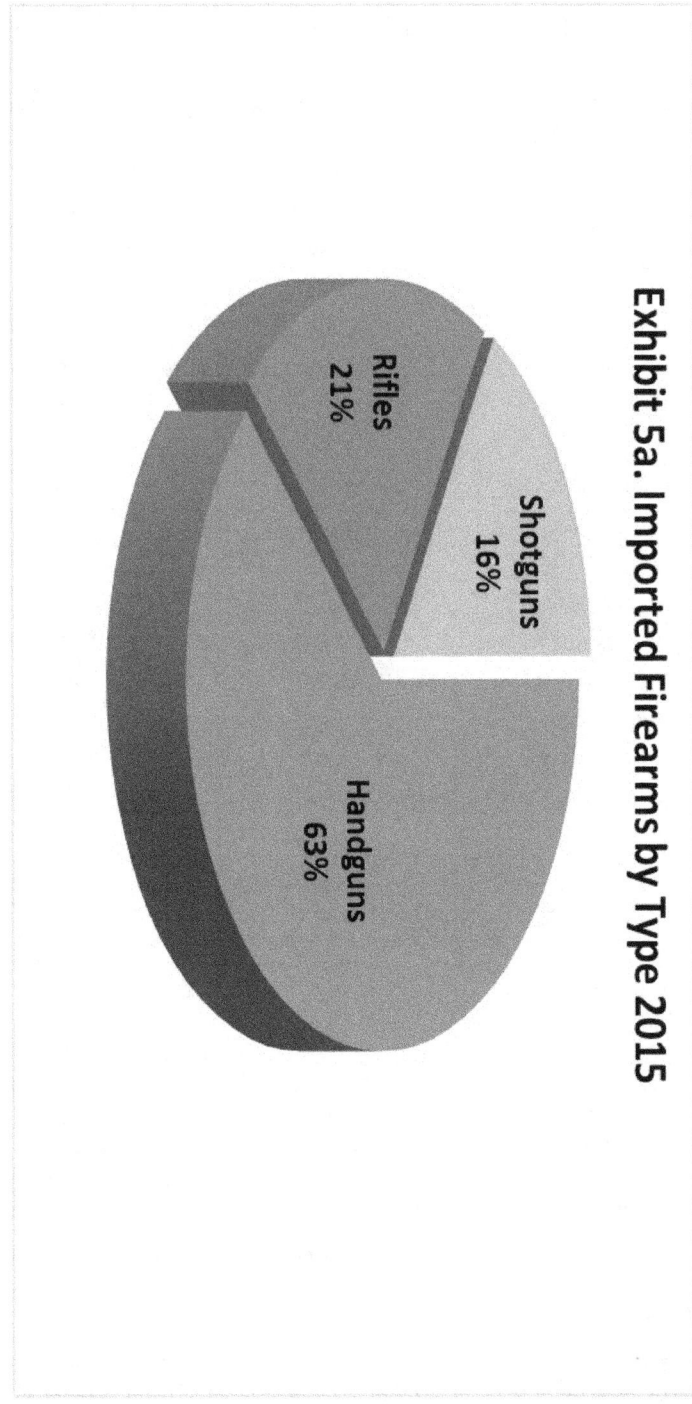

Exhibit 5a. Imported Firearms by Type 2015

Rifles
21%

Shotguns
16%

Handguns
63%

Exhibit 6. National Firearms Act Tax Revenues and Related Activities
(1984 - 2015)

Fiscal Year[1]	Occupational Tax Paid[2]	Transfer and Making Tax Paid	Enforcement Supp	
			Certifications	Records Checks
1984	$596,000	$666,000	1,196	2,771
1985	$606,000	$594,000	921	3,682
1986	$667,000	$1,372,000	690	3,376
1987	$869,000	$1,576,000	575	4,135
1988	$2,095,000	$1,481,000	701	3,738
1989	$1,560,000	$1,527,000	1,196	6,128
1990	$1,442,000	$1,308,000	666	7,981
1991	$1,556,000	$1,210,000	764	7,857
1992	$1,499,000	$1,237,000	1,257	8,582
1993	$1,493,000	$1,264,000	1,024	7,230
1994	$1,444,000	$1,596,000	586	6,283
1995	$1,007,000	$1,311,000	882	5,677
1996	$1,143,000	$1,402,000	529	5,215
1997	$1,284,000	$1,630,000	488	4,395
1998	$1,299,000	$1,969,000	353	3,824
1999	$1,330,000	$2,422,000	345	3,994
2000	$1,399,000	$2,301,000	144	2,159
2001	$1,456,000	$2,800,000	402	5,156
2002	$1,492,000	$1,510,000	441	6,381
2003	$1,758,000	$2,699,000	401	6,597
2004	$1,640,000	$3,052,000	435	6,191
2005	$1,659,000	$2,810,000	447	6,218
2006	$1,709,000	$3,951,000	327	6,331
2007	$1,815,000	$4,890,000	530	7,468
2008	$1,950,000	$5,742,000	375	5,872
2009	$2,125,000	$7,971,000	418	5,736
2010	$2,530,000	$7,184,000	267	5,883
2011	$2,952,000	$9,576,000	287	6,313
2012	$3,628,000	$12,814,000	390	7,103
2013	$4,294,000	$18,182,000	501	7,138
2014	$4,837,000	$22,678,000	367	6,172
2015	$5,417,000	$32,462,000	338	5,650

Source: ATF's National Firearms Registration and Transfer Record (NFRTR).

[1]Data from 1997 - 2000 were based on calendar year data.

[2]Special occupational tax revenues for FY 1990 - 1996 include collections made during the fiscal year for prior tax years. Importers, manufacturers, or dealers in NFA firearms are subject to a yearly occupational tax.

[3]ATF searches the NFRTR in support of criminal investigations and regulatory inspections in order to determine whether persons are legally in possession of NFA weapons and whether transfers are made lawfully.

Data from 2000-2010 for Certifications and Records Checks was corrected in the 2012 update.

Exhibit 7. National Firearms Act Firearms Processed by Form Type
(1990 - 2015)

Calendar Year[1]	Application to Make NFA Firearms (ATF Form 1)	Manufactured and Imported (ATF Form 2)	Application for Tax Exempt Transfer Between Licensees (ATF Form 3)	Application for Taxpaid Transfer (ATF Form 4)	Application for Tax-Exempt Transfer[2] (ATF Form 5)	Exported (ATF Form 9)	Total[3]
1990	399	66,084	23,149	7,024	54,959	21,725	173,340
1991	524	80,619	19,507	5,395	44,146	40,387	190,578
1992	351	107,313	26,352	6,541	45,390	22,120	208,067
1993	310	70,342	22,071	7,388	60,193	24,041	184,345
1994	1,076	97,665	27,950	7,600	67,580	34,242	236,113
1995	1,226	95,061	18,593	8,263	60,055	31,258	214,456
1996	1,174	103,511	16,931	6,418	72,395	40,439	240,868
1997	855	110,423	18,371	7,873	70,690	36,284	244,496
1998	1,093	141,101	27,921	10,181	93,135	40,221	313,652
1999	1,071	137,373	28,288	11,768	95,554	28,128	302,182
2000	1,334	141,763	23,335	11,246	96,234	28,672	302,584
2001	2,522	145,112	25,745	10,799	101,955	25,759	311,892
2002	1,173	162,321	25,042	10,686	92,986	47,597	339,805
2003	1,003	156,620	21,936	13,501	107,108	43,668	343,836
2004	980	83,483	20,026	14,635	54,675	19,425	193,224
2005	1,902	65,865	26,603	14,606	26,210	20,951	156,137
2006	2,610	188,134	51,290	20,534	100,458	42,175	405,201
2007	3,553	296,267	51,217	22,260	194,794	76,467	644,558
2008	4,583	424,743	71,404	26,917	183,271	206,411	917,329
2009	5,345	371,920	56,947	31,551	201,267	163,951	830,981
2010	5,169	296,375	58,875	33,059	189,449	136,335	719,262
2011	5,477	530,953	107,066	33,816	147,341	311,214	1,135,867
2012	7,886	484,928	149,762	52,490	170,561	219,700	1,085,327
2013	9,347	477,567	206,389	57,294	110,637	224,515	1,085,749
2014	22,380	591,388	262,342	107,921	138,204	248,109	1,370,344
2015	32,558	583,499	365,791	130,017	127,945	306,037	1,545,847

Source: ATF's National Firearms Registration and Transfer Record (NFRTR).

[1]Data from 1990 - 1996 represent fiscal year.

[2]Firearms may be transferred to the U.S., State or local governments without the payment of a transfer tax. Further transfers of NFA firearms between licensees registered as importers, manufacturers, or dealers who have paid the special occupational tax are likewise exempt from transfer tax.

[3]Totals do not include ATF Form 5320.20 or ATF Form 10 because these do not relate to commercial transactions.

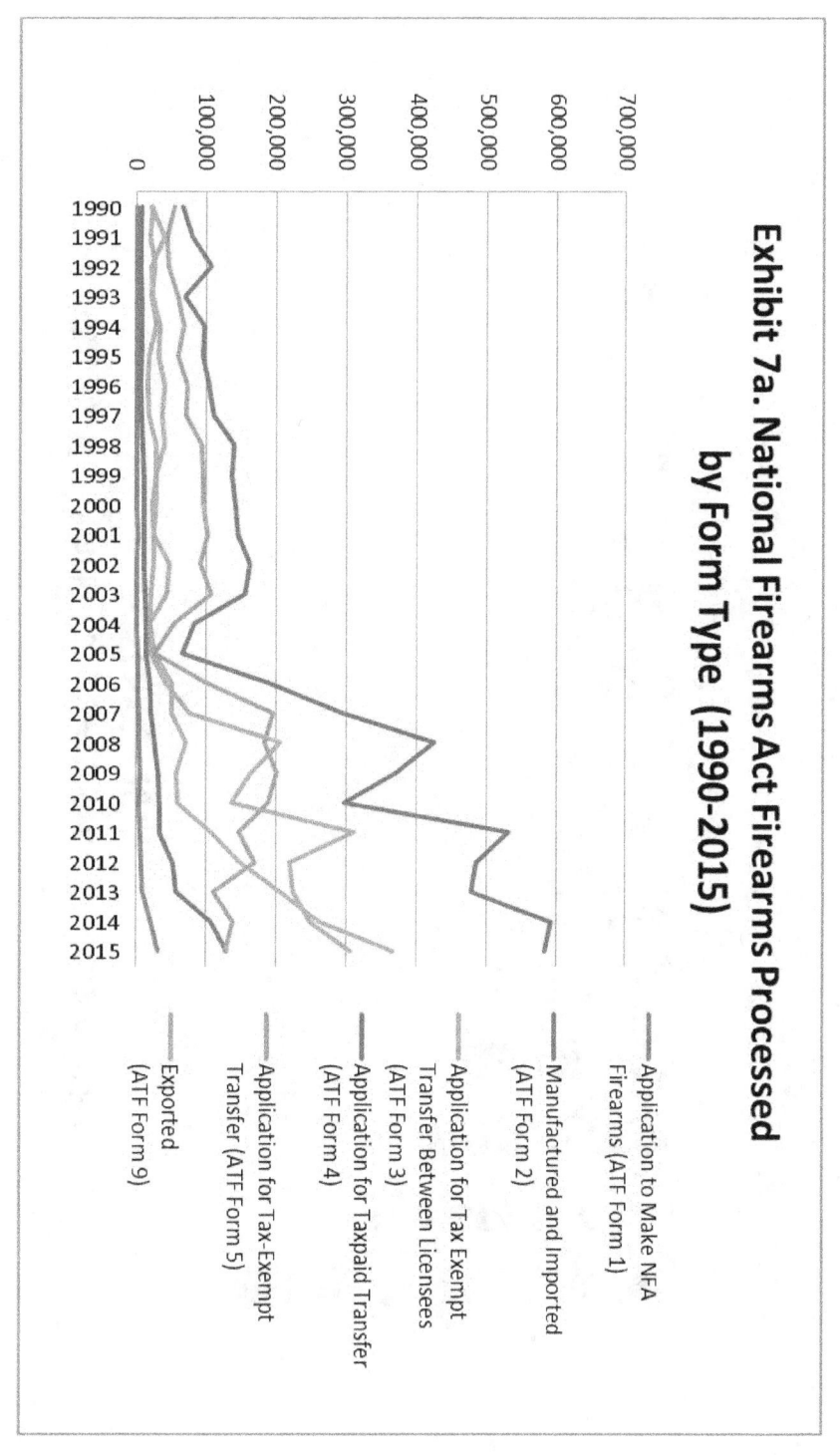

Exhibit 7a. National Firearms Act Firearms Processed by Form Type (1990-2015)

Application to Make NFA Firearms (ATF Form 1)

Manufactured and Imported (ATF Form 2)

Application for Tax Exempt Transfer Between Licensees (ATF Form 3)

Application for Taxpaid Transfer (ATF Form 4)

Application for Tax-Exempt Transfer (ATF Form 5)

Exported (ATF Form 9)

13

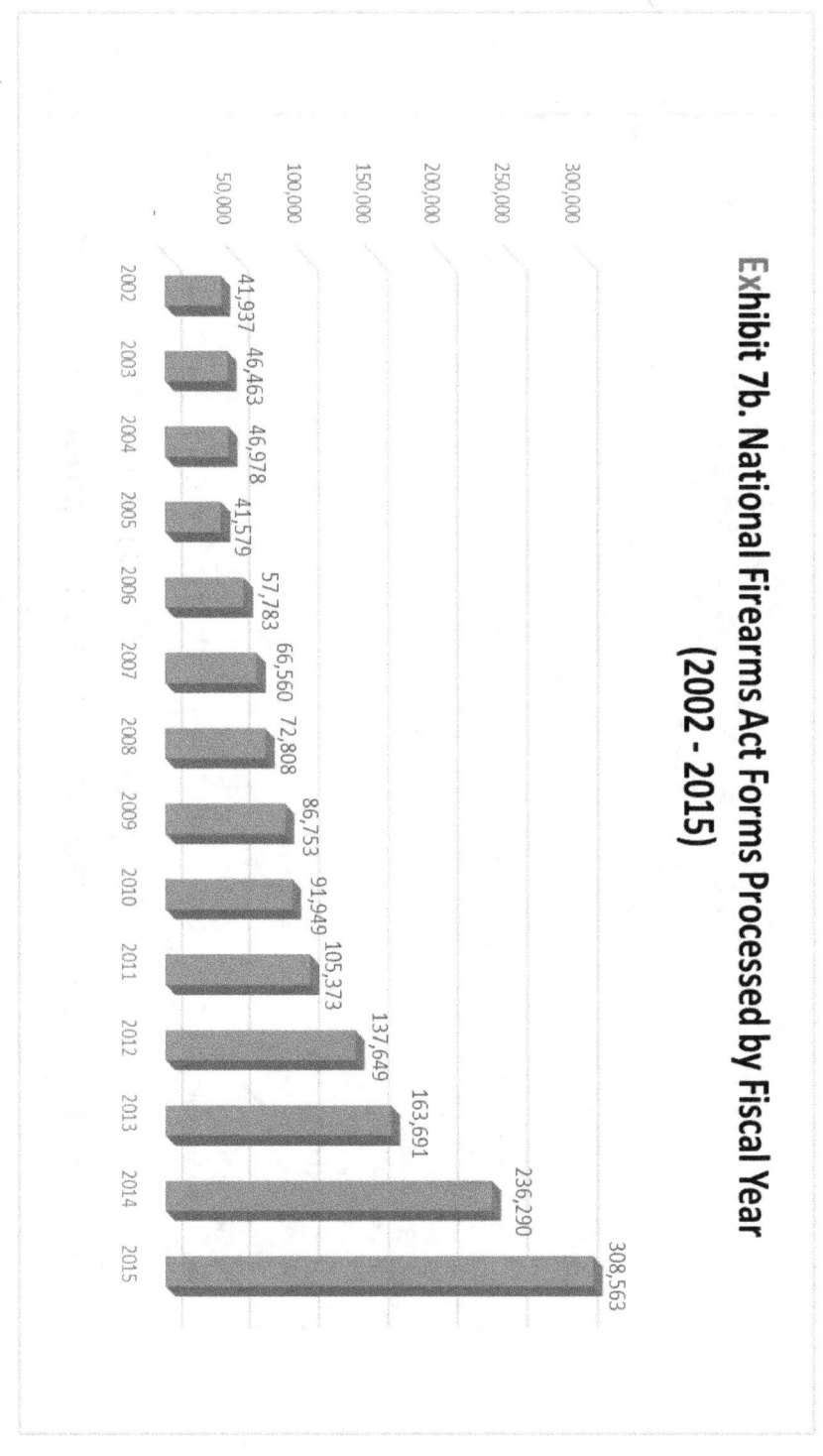

Exhibit 7b. National Firearms Act Forms Processed by Fiscal Year (2002 - 2015)

Year	Value
2002	41,937
2003	46,463
2004	46,978
2005	41,579
2006	57,783
2007	66,560
2008	72,808
2009	86,753
2010	91,949
2011	105,373
2012	137,649
2013	163,691
2014	236,290
2015	308,563

14

Exhibit 8. National Firearms Act Registered Weapons by State (Feb 2016)

State	Any Other Weapon[1]	Destructive Device[2]	Machinegun[3]	Silencer[4]	Short Barreled Rifle[5]	Short Barreled Shotgun[6]	Total
Alabama	1,166	77,283	19,390	30,849	3,765	2,234	134,687
Alaska	322	4,651	1,652	4,213	1,333	1,268	13,439
Arkansas	604	45,813	5,189	14,370	2,464	1,060	69,500
Arizona	1,185	86,309	16,318	28,942	10,351	2,143	145,248
California	3,884	256,420	29,516	11,702	9,472	13,423	324,417
Colorado	961	44,598	7,111	18,689	4,859	1,660	77,878
Connecticut	708	12,220	37,939	8,352	3,374	983	63,576
District of Columbia	69	39,134	4,496	308	787	1,101	45,895
Delaware	32	2,748	583	324	184	537	4,408
Florida	3,448	151,672	34,373	61,015	18,409	8,310	277,227
Georgia	1,929	66,433	28,497	49,357	8,132	11,175	165,523
Hawaii	34	6,863	410	143	59	62	7,571
Iowa	876	15,398	3,495	983	521	965	22,238
Idaho	641	17,172	4,039	18,176	2,437	459	42,924
Illinois	979	101,572	30,563	1,717	2,278	1,716	138,825
Indiana	1,615	41,343	18,880	28,395	4,709	8,816	103,758
Kansas	704	22,580	3,667	7,715	2,276	966	37,908
Kentucky	1,088	30,580	13,568	22,238	2,914	1,811	72,199
Louisiana	543	51,268	6,686	25,203	3,603	1,712	89,015
Massachusetts	831	15,028	6,705	6,772	2,312	981	32,629
Maryland	998	49,865	26,074	12,340	4,102	4,068	97,447
Maine	578	3,320	4,858	2,467	1,725	454	13,402
Michigan	1,155	24,561	12,913	10,146	2,203	1,244	52,222
Minnesota	2,654	42,890	9,264	5,655	2,404	1,132	63,999
Missouri	1,378	30,433	9,472	15,052	4,080	2,499	62,914
Mississippi	426	9,628	4,220	10,589	1,747	798	27,408
Montana	444	3,675	2,373	7,928	1,042	438	15,900
North Carolina	922	84,705	11,947	24,346	6,697	2,922	131,539
North Dakota	204	1,926	1,581	4,836	642	271	9,460
Nebraska	763	6,291	2,217	6,576	1,354	810	18,011
New Hampshire	447	4,253	9,325	12,120	3,194	482	29,821
New Jersey	426	42,674	7,730	1,130	1,144	2,568	55,672
New Mexico	302	79,180	3,847	6,159	2,080	683	92,251
Nevada	812	35,251	10,336	14,928	5,504	954	67,785
New York	1,632	41,055	12,210	3,466	4,594	7,449	70,406
Ohio	1,872	78,639	19,952	30,714	6,137	5,920	143,234
Oklahoma	1,169	16,087	9,136	32,192	3,804	1,675	64,063
Oregon	1,549	20,825	6,415	17,537	4,158	1,439	51,923
Pennsylvania	2,115	152,262	17,989	29,742	7,779	12,835	222,722
Rhode Island	41	3,187	639	29	119	113	4,128
South Carolina	678	33,365	8,302	23,451	3,495	3,922	73,213
South Dakota	352	3,761	1,718	7,320	547	194	13,892
Tennessee	1,599	40,466	13,855	19,736	5,438	6,010	87,104
Texas	6,740	224,498	34,848	165,499	29,509	7,487	468,581
Utah	455	16,117	6,699	26,039	3,725	1,332	54,367
Virginia	2,854	193,728	33,199	31,205	12,665	7,705	281,356
Vermont	223	2,548	1,122	405	295	130	4,723
Washington	1,855	43,287	4,229	21,797	3,967	822	75,957
Wisconsin	760	30,096	7,292	11,156	3,169	1,224	53,697
West Virginia	446	16,928	6,774	5,020	1,349	1,023	31,540
Wyoming	303	120,899	1,774	3,744	675	392	127,787
Other US Territories	6	359	215	18	12	97	707
Total	57,777	2,545,844	575,602	902,805	213,594	140,474	4,436,096

Source: ATF National Firearms Registration and Transfer Record (NFRTR).

[1] The term "any other weapon" means any weapon or device capable of being concealed on the person from which a shot can be discharged through the energy of an explosive, a pistol or revolver having a barrel with a smooth bore designed or redesigned to fire a fixed shotgun shell, weapons with combination shotgun and rifle barrels 12 inches or more, less than 18 inches in length, from which only a single discharge can be made from either barrel without manual reloading, and shall include any such weapon which may be readily restored to fire. Such term shall not include a pistol or a revolver having a rifled bore, or rifled bores, or weapons designed, made, or intended to be fired from the shoulder and not capable of firing fixed ammunition.

[2] Destructive device generally is defined as (a) Any explosive, incendiary, or poison gas (1) bomb, (2) grenade, (3) rocket having a propellant charge of more than 4 ounces, (4) missile having an explosive or incendiary charge of more than one-quarter ounce, (5) mine, or (6) device similar to any of the devices described in the preceding paragraphs of this definition; (b) any type of weapon (other than a shotgun or a shotgun shell which the Director finds is generally recognized as particularly suitable for sporting purposes) by whatever name known which will, or which may be readily converted to, expel a projectile by the action of an explosive or other propellant, and which has any barrel with a bore of more than one-half inch in diameter; and (c) any combination of parts either designed or intended for use in converting any device into any destructive device described in paragraph (a) or (b) of this section and from which a destructive device may be readily assembled. The term shall not include any device which is neither designed nor redesigned for use as a weapon; any device, although originally designed for use as a weapon, which is redesigned for use as a signaling, pyrotechnic, line throwing, safety, or similar device; surplus ordnance sold, loaned, or given by the Secretary of the Army pursuant to the provisions of section 4684(2), 4685, or 4686 of title 10, United States Code; or any other device which the Director finds is not likely to be used as a weapon, is an antique, or is a rifle which the owner intends to use solely for sporting, recreational, or cultural purposes.

[3] Machinegun is defined as any weapon which shoots, is designed to shoot, or can be readily restored to shoot, automatically more than one shot, without manual reloading, by a single function of the trigger. The term shall also include the frame or receiver of any such weapon, any part designed and intended solely and exclusively, or combination of parts designed and intended, for use in converting a weapon into a machinegun, and any combination of parts from which a machinegun can be assembled if such parts are in the possession or under the control of a person.

[4] Silencer is defined as any device for silencing, muffling, or diminishing the report of a portable firearm, including any combination of parts, designed or redesigned, and intended for the use in assembling or fabricating a firearm silencer or firearm muffler, and any part intended only for use in such assembly or fabrication.

[5] Short-barreled rifle is defined as a rifle having one or more barrels less than 16 inches in length, and any weapon made from a rifle, whether by alteration, modification, or otherwise, if such weapon, as modified, has an overall length of less than 26 inches.

[6] Short-barreled shotgun is defined as a shotgun having one or more barrels less than 18 inches in length, and any weapon made from a shotgun, whether by alteration, modification, or otherwise, if such weapon as modified has an overall length of less than 26 inches.

Exhibit 9. National Firearms Act Special Occupational Taxpayers by State
Tax Year 2015

State	Importers	Manufacturers	Dealers	Total
Alabama	21	87	77	185
Alaska	0	19	36	55
Arizona	25	298	166	489
Arkansas	13	79	77	169
California	10	106	85	201
Colorado	3	102	117	222
Connecticut	8	58	35	101
Delaware	0	0	1	1
District of Columbia	0	0	1	1
Florida	51	299	372	722
Georgia	9	131	206	346
Hawaii	0	0	1	1
Idaho	2	30	25	57
Illinois	1	85	59	145
Indiana	8	59	30	97
Iowa	1	89	139	229
Kansas	5	36	81	122
Kentucky	14	73	109	196
Louisiana	1	65	113	179
Maine	3	26	31	60
Maryland	7	55	66	128
Massachusetts	3	66	23	92
Michigan	6	68	120	194
Minnesota	12	80	42	134
Mississippi	6	49	65	120
Missouri	12	110	140	262
Montana	2	34	55	91
Nebraska	0	28	37	65
Nevada	7	111	69	187
New Hampshire	6	62	42	110
New Jersey	1	6	15	22
New Mexico	9	58	49	116
New York	2	41	17	60
North Carolina	2	139	202	343
North Dakota	0	7	25	32
Ohio	2	156	175	333
Oklahoma	0	98	107	205
Oregon	2	90	107	199
Pennsylvania	17	138	211	366
Rhode Island	1	1	1	3
South Carolina	6	63	81	150
South Dakota	1	25	49	75
Tennessee	4	97	132	233
Texas	40	470	693	1203
Utah	1	70	67	138
Vermont	4	14	5	23
Virginia	44	136	195	375
Washington	5	87	80	172
West Virginia	7	37	57	101
Wisconsin	10	92	72	174
Wyoming	2	26	37	65
Total	396	4,156	4,797	9,349

Source: ATF's National Firearms Act Special Occupational Tax Database (NSOT)

Numbers represent qualified premises locations.

Exhibit 10. Federal Firearms Licensees Total (1975-2015)

| Fiscal Year | Dealer | Pawn-broker | Collector | Manufacturer of | | Importer | Destructive Device | | | Total |
				Ammunition	Firearms		Dealer	Manufacturer	Importer	
1975	146,429	2,813	5,211	6,668	364	403	9	23	7	161,927
1976	150,767	2,882	4,036	7,181	397	403	4	19	8	165,697
1977	157,463	2,943	4,446	7,761	408	419	6	28	10	173,484
1978	152,681	3,113	4,629	7,735	422	417	6	35	14	169,052
1979	153,861	3,388	4,975	8,055	459	426	7	33	12	171,216
1980	155,690	3,608	5,481	8,856	496	430	7	40	11	174,619
1981	168,301	4,308	6,490	10,067	540	519	7	44	20	190,296
1982	184,840	5,002	8,602	12,033	675	676	12	54	24	211,918
1983	200,342	5,388	9,859	13,318	788	795	16	71	36	230,613
1984	195,847	5,140	8,643	11,270	710	704	15	74	40	222,443
1985	219,366	6,207	9,599	11,818	778	881	15	85	45	248,794
1986	235,393	6,998	10,639	12,095	843	1,035	16	95	52	267,166
1987	230,888	7,316	11,094	10,613	852	1,084	16	101	58	262,022
1988	239,637	8,261	12,638	10,169	926	1,123	18	112	69	272,953
1989	231,442	8,626	13,536	8,345	922	989	21	110	72	264,063
1990	235,684	9,029	14,287	7,945	978	946	20	117	73	269,079
1991	241,706	9,625	15,143	7,470	1,059	901	17	120	75	276,116
1992	248,155	10,452	15,820	7,412	1,165	894	15	127	77	284,117
1993	246,984	10,958	16,635	6,947	1,256	924	15	128	78	283,925
1994	213,734	10,872	17,690	6,068	1,302	963	12	122	70	250,833
1995	158,240	10,155	16,354	4,459	1,242	842	14	118	71	191,495
1996	105,398	9,974	14,966	3,144	1,327	786	12	117	70	135,794
1997	79,285	9,956	13,512	2,451	1,414	733	13	118	72	107,554
1998	75,619	10,176	14,875	2,374	1,546	741	12	125	68	105,536
1999	71,290	10,035	17,763	2,247	1,639	755	11	127	75	103,942
2000	67,479	9,737	21,100	2,112	1,773	748	12	125	71	103,157
2001	63,845	9,199	25,145	1,950	1,841	730	14	117	72	102,913
2002	59,829	8,770	30,157	1,763	1,941	735	16	126	74	103,411
2003	57,492	8,521	33,406	1,693	2,046	719	16	130	82	104,105
2004	56,103	8,180	37,206	1,625	2,144	720	16	136	84	106,214
2005	53,833	7,809	40,073	1,502	2,272	696	15	145	87	106,432
2006	51,462	7,386	43,650	1,431	2,411	690	17	170	99	107,316
2007	49,221	6,966	47,690	1,399	2,668	686	23	174	106	108,933
2008	48,261	6,687	52,597	1,420	2,959	688	29	189	113	112,943
2009	47,509	6,675	55,046	1,511	3,543	735	34	215	127	115,395
2010	47,664	6,895	56,680	1,759	4,293	768	40	243	145	118,487
2011	48,676	7,075	59,227	1,895	5,441	811	42	259	161	123,587
2012	50,848	7,426	61,885	2,044	7,423	848	52	261	169	130,956
2013	54,026	7,810	64,449	2,353	9,094	998	57	273	184	139,244
2014	55,431	8,132	63,301	2,596	9,970	1,133	66	287	200	141,116
2015	56,181	8,152	60,652	2,603	10,498	1,152	66	315	221	139,840

Source: ATF Federal Firearms Licensing Center, Federal Licensing System (FLS). Data is based on active firearms licenses and related statistics as of the end of each fiscal year.

Exhibit 11. Federal Firearms Licensees by State 2015

State	FFL Population
Alabama	2,385
Alaska	952
Arizona	3,202
Arkansas	2,018
California	8,261
Colorado	2,967
Connecticut	1,826
Delaware	340
District of Columbia	28
Florida	7,507
Georgia	3,807
Hawaii	288
Idaho	1,429
Illinois	5,295
Indiana	2,994
Iowa	2,172
Kansas	1,952
Kentucky	2,507
Louisiana	2,176
Maine	967
Maryland	3,417
Massachusetts	4,039
Michigan	4,262
Minnesota	2,676
Mississippi	1,560
Missouri	5,091
Montana	1,543
Nebraska	1,165
Nevada	1,368
New Hampshire	1,187
New Jersey	550
New Mexico	1,154
New York	4,081
North Carolina	4,819
North Dakota	666
Ohio	5,027
Oklahoma	2,483
Oregon	2,481
Pennsylvania	6,347
Rhode Island	610
South Carolina	2,240
South Dakota	803
Tennessee	3,482
Texas	10,910
Utah	1,361
Vermont	551
Virginia	4,374
Washington	2,857
West Virginia	1,497
Wisconsin	3,141
Wyoming	901
Other Territories	124
Total	139,840

Source: ATF, Federal Firearms Licensing Center, Firearms Licensing System. Data is based on active firearms licenses and related statistics as of the end of the fiscal year.

Exhibit 12. Actions on Federal Firearms License Applications (1975 - 2015)

Fiscal Year	Original Application Processed	Denied	Withdrawn[1]	Abandoned[2]
1975	29,183	150	1,651	...
1976	29,511	209	2,077	
1977	32,560	216	1,645	...
1978	29,531	151	1,015	414
1979	32,678	124	432	433
1980	36,052	96	601	661
1981	41,798	85	742	329
1982	44,745	52	580	370
1983	49,669	151	916	649
1984	39,321	98	706	833
1985	37,385	103	666	598
1986	42,842	299	698	452
1987	36,835	121	874	458
1988	32,724	30	506	315
1989	34,318	34	561	360
1990	34,336	46	893	404
1991	34,567	37	1,059	685
1992	37,085	57	1,337	611
1993	41,545	343	6,030	1,844
1994	25,393	136	4,480	3,917
1995	7,777	49	1,046	1,180
1996	8,461	58	1,061	629
1997	7,039	24	692	366
1998	7,090	19	621	352
1999	8,581	23	48	298
2000	10,698	6	447	91
2001	11,161	3	403	114
2002	16,100	13	468	175
2003	13,884	30	729	289
2004	12,953	18	572	235
2005	13,326	33	943	300
2006	13,757	35	898	234
2007	14,123	32	953	402
2008	15,434	21	1,030	291
2009	16,105	20	1,415	724
2010	16,930	32	1,467	380
2011	19,923	22	1,744	369
2012	20,977	28	2,252	358
2013	23,242	30	2,901	385
2014	17,816	27	2,192	444
2015	15,219	34	1,953	387

Source: ATF

[1]An application can be withdrawn by an applicant at any time prior to the issuance of a license.

[2]If ATF cannot locate an applicant during an attempted application inspection or cannot obtain needed verification data, then the application will be abandoned.

Exhibit 13. Federal Firearms Licensees and Compliance Inspections
(FY 1975-2015)

Fiscal Year	Inspections	Total Licensees	Percent Inspected	Licensed Business Entities[1]	Percent Inspected
1975	10,944	161,927	6.7%	156,716	7.0%
1976	15,171	165,697	9.1%	161,661	9.4%
1977	19,741	173,484	11.3%	169,038	11.7%
1978	22,130	169,052	13.1%	164,423	13.5%
1979	14,744	171,216	8.6%	166,241	8.9%
1980	11,515	174,619	6.5%	169,138	6.8%
1981	11,035	190,296	5.7%	183,806	6.0%
1982	1,829	211,918	0.8%	203,316	0.9%
1983	2,662	230,613	1.1%	220,754	1.2%
1984	8,861	222,443	3.9%	213,800	4.1%
1985	9,527	248,794	3.8%	239,195	4.0%
1986	8,605	267,166	3.2%	256,527	3.4%
1987	8,049	262,022	3.1%	250,928	3.2%
1988	9,283	272,953	3.4%	260,315	3.6%
1989	7,142	264,063	2.7%	250,527	2.9%
1990	8,471	269,079	3.1%	254,792	3.3%
1991	8,258	276,116	3.0%	260,973	3.2%
1992	16,328	284,117	5.7%	268,297	6.1%
1993	22,330	283,925	7.9%	267,290	8.4%
1994	20,067	250,833	8.0%	233,143	8.6%
1995	13,141	191,495	7.0%	171,577	7.7%
1996	10,051	135,794	7.4%	120,828	8.3%
1997	5,925	107,554	5.5%	94,042	6.3%
1998	5,043	105,536	4.8%	90,661	5.6%
1999	9,004	103,942	8.7%	86,179	10.4%
2000	3,640	103,157	3.5%	82,558	4.4%
2001	3,677	102,913	3.6%	77,768	4.7%
2002	5,467	103,411	5.2%	73,254	7.5%
2003	5,170	104,105	4.9%	70,699	7.3%
2004	4,509	106,214	4.2%	69,008	6.5%
2005	5,189	106,432	4.9%	66,359	7.8%
2006	7,294	107,316	6.8%	63,666	11.5%
2007	10,141	108,933	9.3%	61,243	16.6%
2008	11,100	112,943	9.8%	60,346	18.4%
2009	11,375	115,395	9.9%	60,349	18.8%
2010	10,538	118,487	8.9%	61,807	17.0%
2011	13,159	123,587	10.6%	64,360	20.4%
2012	11,420	130,956	8.7%	69,071	16.5%
2013	10,516	139,244	7.6%	74,795	14.1%
2014	10,437	141,116	7.4%	77,815	13.4%
2015	8,696	139,840	6.3%	79,188	11.0%

Source: ATF

[1] Does not include Collector of Curio and Relics (Type 03)

www.ingramcontent.com/pod-product-compliance
Lightning Source LLC
Chambersburg PA
CBHW081547280526
45788CB00010B/3388